Becoming the Difference in a Hopeful Classroom

By:

Felicia Saffold

ISBN: 1512315516
ISBN-13: 978-1512315516

3 | Becoming the Difference in a Hopeful Classroom

CONTENTS

5 | Becoming the Difference in a Hopeful Classroom

INTRODUCTION

Since I was a child, I loved being in school. I loved to learn, and this is one of the reasons why it came as no surprise to anyone that I wanted to be a teacher. Educating someone else was my vision, and I could see that goal so clearly. When the days would wind down, and the clock ticked closer to summer vacation, I was the student sitting in class wishing it was the beginning of the school year, instead of the end. I loved everything about the classroom. I loved the loud noises that could be heard before the bell would ring, the pencil sharpener making its all-too-familiar churning sound, and everything in between. Each morning I would wake up yearning for that feeling; a feeling that I could only receive as I walked through the hallways of the school building with my peers. Each day was like a new adventure for me, and every

morning I would race to school so that I could walk through
the doors, anxiously anticipating a new journey.

Some days I would enter the school and wonder what we
would learn today. If the lesson was not up-to-par with what
I had in mind, I would wait until later that evening and
recreate the classroom at home. I actually held class in my
own backyard. Some of the children who were younger than
me would need help; therefore, they could come and have an
educational session or two with me each day. There is a
feeling that I find difficult to describe when it pertains to
helping others learn. If I had to choose a superlative, I would
use the word "magical." Teaching was magical to me. I was
in awe with what we, as individuals full of knowledge, could
teach; I was equally enamored by what we could learn as a
student.

I do not want to sound like an extremely rare person who
walked the halls in a fictional book, racing to class each day,
because I was not. It was not the class that had my full love
and devotion; I was in love with school. Some of my teachers

and classes were extremely boring, but that did not bother me at all. In fact, regardless of how boring a class may have been, the thought of learning made each class worth attending. The thing that made school appealing to me was when my teachers allowed us students to learn in a fun way. For instance, one day my seventh grade social studies teacher allowed us to create our own country in class. I remember it like it happened yesterday; the name of my group was known as "Candy Land." Just about everyone in the world should be familiar with this board game, referred to as Candy Land. The game allowed players to go from one delicious destination to another. Each adventure in Candy Land was sweet, and I wanted my country to be just as tasteful; hence the name Candy Land.

This was a pivotal time in my life. It was at this actual moment that I knew I wanted to be a teacher. Every other moment that I had experienced paled in comparison to this moment right here. Learning for me had finally come to life, and I knew that the only job I would want to take on would be that of an educator. I did not long for the bright lights and the crowd cheering my name. Fame, fortune, and glamour were not as fascinating to me as helping someone learn. The only crowd that I wanted to hear cheering for me was a crowd filled with students who had learned, parents who were proud of the educational system that uplifted their children, and the cheering of other teachers who were in awe of my exceptional teaching skills.

Yes, creating and designing my own group as a seventh grader had inspired me to be the teacher that I am today. I thought about the children who would love my class, and how the students would brag to other students within the school. Soon, every student would know my name and wish to be inside of my classroom. This was the rock-star that I wanted to be; a teacher who was known amongst the students and school staff as a rock-star. The teacher who made learning fun; a teacher that taught a class everyone wanted to be a part of. Even though the students would learn about my great reputation through their peers, I knew that each child would genuinely want to be a part of my classroom – they would be there because they actually wanted to be there. My students would learn because they wanted to learn.

It was at this moment that I realized being a teacher was my only option. Sure there were countless opportunities that awaited me, such as becoming a doctor, lawyer, business owner, and so on; however, this was the only career option that I wanted, and I would achieve it. I wanted to watch my students light up with excitement as they learned history, mathematics, language arts, science, and other required subject matter. I wanted to see the love displayed on their faces as they realized that learning could actually be fun, just like I had at that very moment in my seventh grade social studies class. That was an experience that I have never had, and I knew from that day forth, teaching was it for me, and it was all that I would aspire to do.

I would one day walk into a classroom that was my own… My very own Candy Land!

CHAPTER 1:

OFF TO TEACH ... UNEXPECTED REALITIES

"To expect the unexpected shows a thoroughly modern intellect." – Oscar Wilde

Here I was, well over a decade later, beginning my first official day as a new teacher. I remember thinking why would a new teacher be hired during the middle of a school semester – it was January. This was not typical with teaching assignments, but I was so excited about being offered my first teaching position that I accepted it without any thought. However, it was not long before I started to question the offer.

A picture is said to be worth a thousand words, but my current view was nothing like the Candy Land I had created in my mind over and over again; instead, it seemed lifeless. I had not expected cotton candy and other treats, but I expected to see anything but this.

I had arrived an hour prior to the school day beginning, ready to take on my new adventure. As I was driving through the neighborhood, I noticed that it was not the greatest scenery. I knew that teaching in an urban public school would not be the same as teaching in a privileged community. However, I did not become a teacher to be employed by the wealthiest school located in an affluent neighborhood. I wanted to be the difference; I wanted to make a difference. So many teachers – even those who come from underprivileged schools – leave in search of the school system that seems "flawless." This is a myth, because the students are generally what determine the flaws within the school. Regardless if a school system has the best computer system, and the greatest learning materials, the students can be flawed. Being flawed is not a bad thing – in my eyes, but to many, it could be the deciding factor as to if a position is accepted or not.

Going back to my dreams, I knew that what I was going to experience on my first day as a teacher was extremely different, when compared to those dreams. Yet and still, as I stepped into the halls of my first school placement, I was full of excitement. This was it; the moment that I had been waiting for. My mind quickly drifted back to my seventh grade year in social studies class. I was able to create a country as a part of my class assignment, but on this very day, I would be creating my own class. I would develop a fun learning environment that my students would love. Hopefully my lessons would inspire one of my students to become a teacher, and the dream would continue.

I did not expect to be greeted at the door with roses and balloons, but a little common courtesy would have been nice. If the principal could not welcome me to the school, perhaps a vice principal would be there, right? Wrong! I was completely shocked when no one came to the door to welcome me. Even so, I was confident that an administrator or staff member would help me become acquainted with my class. Surely someone would introduce me to my class and wait until I was settled in to leave. Again, I was wrong… well, somewhat. I was handed a stack of books and the keys to my classroom by a secretary who was extremely rude. Monday is not the most popular day of the week, but a little more cheer would have been appreciated. Instead, the secretary pointed toward the elevator, and told me that my class was located on the third floor. That was it; no grand affair. Moment by moment, Candy Land was drifting further and further away.

Suddenly, those statistics that I learned while in college were now flashing back into my mind. More than 200,000 new teachers are hired in the United States each year, and of those teachers, nearly half leave the profession within five years. I remembered reading those stats and thinking, why would anyone go through at least four years of college, followed by student teaching and certification, only to quit? That was senseless, right? Then there was the fact that this type of action costs the nation's school districts approximately 7.2 billion dollars each year. This was money that could help millions of students, especially those in urban school districts that are already understaffed and have limited learning resources. I remember thinking that would never be me. I would not let the educational system down, and I would not fail my students. I wanted to help bring something great into the classroom. I truly believed that I, along with countless other teachers around the country, could help transform the school systems, one class at a time.

I was determined to make this day the best day ever. I could not let the excitement that I had built up over the years go without putting up a fight. I did not have to do much fighting as I walked to my classroom. I felt that feeling again; suddenly, I was a kid in class as I grabbed for the keys to my classroom door. Every test, every assignment, every lecture, every chapter I read, and all of the other obstacles I had faced on my journey to become a certified teacher were worth it. I was going to unlock the door to my very own classroom. This is the moment that dreams were made of, and I refused to let anyone – or anything – ruin this moment for me. I was a young girl all over again, but this time I had my own class, instead of teaching in the yard behind my home.

The word magic was popping around in my mind. This was a truly magical moment that I would never forget. I thought about helping each child one-by-one. I would help my students achieve greatness. I would stress the importance of a solid education, and how regardless of their living or learning environment, my students could be anything that they wanted to be, as long as they worked hard, and studied even harder. I planned on helping each child move to new levels of curiosity and knowledge; through my tutelage, they would experience growth on an entirely new level.

When I turned the keys to that door, the magic disappeared, and reality set in. I was no longer in Candy Land. My feet were planted firmly on the hard floor of a classroom that was in complete disarray. The beautiful colors I had imagined filling my room were replaced with tacky graffiti and walls covered with markings. The desks were not in order; instead, I set my eyes on at least twenty-two desks that needed to be cleaned thoroughly. I did not want to turn and face my teaching desk, but when it was no longer inevitable, I rotated my body and saw the most unattractive desk filled with ditto sheets and unmarked student papers. There were also two large, wooden tables inside of the classroom. These tables looked as if they had been dragged out of an automotive shop, without being dusted off or properly cleaned.

The look of the classroom furniture was atrocious, and the placement of the items did not make the situation any more appealing. I tried to find a pattern, but I was unsuccessful. I could not begin to understand why the room was set up in the manner that it was. As I attempted to walk to my desk, I heard a crunching noise. I stopped, unsure if I wanted to look down, or pretend that I had not heard the noise. The former won, and I looked down at all of the paper that had been crumbled and left on the classroom floor, instead of being placed inside of a waste basket – or recycling bin – where it actually belonged. In addition to the crumpled paper, the floor was decorated with broken pencils, some very old books, and candy wrappers. The latter made me think of Candy Land – helping the dream remain alive, somewhat.

Surely someone knew that I was coming, right? Well of course they did; after all, they hired me. The truth was, they did not care that I was there; they only needed me to be there. The room was a mess, and I could not fathom what the remainder of the day would be like. I sat there for at least five minutes, in complete dismay. To say I was dumbfounded would be an understatement, so I will not.

I quickly realized why the school needed a teacher in the middle of January. This was a job that surely no one wanted, yet I had accepted it without a second thought. I could either continue on, or I could find a way to transfer to a new school. This thought did cross my mind, but then I remembered that it was me who wanted to become a teacher. I thought it would be magical, and I would change the world, one classroom at a time. That was then, and this was now my reality; however, I refused to let what was now in front of me block the dreams that I so eagerly wanted to achieve. I had worked hard for this, my students needed my help, and there was no turning back…

CHAPTER 2:

DEFINING A GOOD TEACHER – DRAWING OUTSIDE OF THE CLASSROOM LINES

"Of all the hard jobs around, one of the hardest is being a good teacher." - Maggie Gallagher

So many new teachers approach being a good educator in the wrong way; teachers are not meant to be the "best-friend" of a student. Yes, teachers need to be relatable, but a teacher's first job is to be that positive educator that the child needs, and deserves. It was not my job to bring frustration into the classroom, regardless of what had happened to me that morning, the day prior, or at any other time period. I could have allowed that first day to keep me from teaching, especially when I actually met my students – more on that in the next chapter.

The truth is that urban schools are in need of a teacher
that not only makes the difference in a child's life, but a
teacher that wants to be the difference in that student's life.
There are various challenges that students attending urban
schools will experience; challenges that students attending a
private school in an upscale community will not. This is in no
way the fault of the student, which is why they should not be
penalized with a less than stellar education. I remember
learning, and enjoying it. The environment did not make me
want to learn, it was the enjoyment that came along with
reading, writing, and all things related to learning. I wanted
the adventure, and each day I woke up anticipating it. My
students would need to receive the type of learning that they
craved, just like I had as a kid. This did not mean I would
"back down" to my students, or try my hardest to be their
"friends." What it meant was that I would go above and
beyond to make sure I helped them earn a solid education,
which was my duty as a teacher – this is true for both veteran
and new teachers, as well as administrators.

I had made tremendous progress with my students since the first day we met. As I looked into the eyes of each student, I saw what they expected from me, and what it was going to take for me to deliver. There was no moment during that first day, and even now, that I did not want to teach my students. Sure, I have had my days that were not as good as others, but that is a part of life – a part of my job. The children in my classroom deserved stability, and I was going to provide that for each of them.

What most new teachers in urban schools do not realize is the challenges that await them once they step foot into the classroom. These challenges may be mentioned here and there while students are in college, but those brief moments do not accurately describe what a teacher will face once they accept a position. The most common challenges that I experienced as a teacher in an urban school were: students were not receiving adequate support from their family or guardians at home; the kids in my classroom had language barriers; and one of the most challenging experiences I had was that some of the children were living with learning disabilities that had not been diagnosed. Even with these issues, I was still in charge of my students while they were in school. It did not matter that they were dealing with issues outside of the classroom that affected their lives inside of the classroom. It was my duty to teach each of my students; that was my job.

Suddenly, teaching students in my backyard seemed simple. Those fourth graders that I "taught" as a young child did not possess any of the challenges that I was now facing as an actual teacher. The children in my neighborhood wanted to learn, and they arrived to my home every session with more desire and determination. Some of the students that I teach in the "real world" do not come into the classroom as eager as others. However, it is my duty to teach every student, regardless if they want to learn or not, right? Wrong! That is exactly the type of thinking that many teachers have. Teaching is not just helping a student learn, it is being the difference in a child's life.

Again, I did not need to be the best friend in my students' lives, but I needed to be the difference. Sometimes being the difference to a child could mean they receive that nurturing and relationship that fills a void, but it is not the responsibility of the teacher to do that. So many children will pass through the classroom of a teacher as the years go by, which makes it extremely important not to get too emotionally attached to the students – sometimes this is easier said than done, but a new teacher has to remain focused.

Well over a decade ago, HBO created a hit fictional series titled *The Wire*. This show focused on the hardships of individuals living in an urban neighborhood that was considered low poverty. The show focused on the criminal activity and gangs within the first few seasons, but during the fourth season of the show, the series focused to school-aged children living in the poverty stricken Baltimore streets. There were four main characters who all had different issues going on within their personal lives, but each of those issues affected each child inside of the classroom. The student's teacher was a white male, in this predominantly black school. He was a former Baltimore police officer who had been demoted, so he decided to use his degree and teach. Out of the four students that the television show focused on, the teacher became extremely attached to one child who had perhaps the worst personal issue… parents who were addicted to drugs.

Like the child in the television series, many students have parents who are addicted to drugs and could care less if their children eat dinner or have a clean living environment. Ensuring that their children make it to school everyday is not even a thought until police officers knock on the door in an attempt to find the children, or serve the parents with a legal summons because their children are truant. These issues are not discussed in college, and new teachers face the challenge of teaching students living in these types of environments on a daily basis.

What I found to be the most interesting is that parents who are addicted to some type of substance truly want better for their children. I noticed that these parents loved their children, but the alcohol and drugs would take over their lives. As a new teacher, I did not have the experience that veteran teachers had, pertaining to helping the parents be more involved in their children's school activities. Experienced teachers understand the benefits that family involvement has on a child's education. Parent involvement has the potential to improve a child's academic performance and mental stability.

Again, the parents love their children, but many are reluctant to be a part of their child's school activities for various reasons. This is not the case with all parents. I found that a majority of the parents want to be active in their children's lives, and they rarely need to be invited to the school; these parents come and check up on their children regularly. However, there are some parents who feel that it is the responsibility of the educational system to teach their children, while others help according to their level of efficacy. If the parent does not feel like he or she could help their child learn, they tend to shy away from doing so. It is out of fear of letting their child down. They are afraid to fail their children. The other reason is they may have their own negative schooling experiences that become barriers to them helping their children. Notice that in all of these reasons, none pertain to how much a parent loves their child; instead, it is circumstance that makes it less likely that a parent will visit class, or participate in school activities.

Some schools are also unwelcoming, which is a huge problem within our society. Parents should be encouraged to attend school functions and community events that help empower their children. It is up to the teachers, school administrators, and community leaders to make parents feel welcome to school events and community activities. When parents need help with personal issues, there needs to be more programs in place that will help the parents. It is also a good idea when teachers make a great effort to include parents. One of the biggest problems for new teachers in urban schools is the fact that these educators lack knowledge and respect of the various ethnicities and cultures of the children that they teach. Taking the time to learn about the

students behind the desk can help teachers learn more about
their families, and how teachers can create plans of action to
keep students motivated, and parents involved.

Returning to the example from the series, *The Wire*...
The teacher in this fictional world would help his students
learn, but he went above his duties by allowing the one child
to come into the school early enough to shower, because the
child's home did not have running water, and his clothes
were never clean. The teacher would wash the child's
uniform each day, and pick up the dirty uniform that the
student would leave each morning as he washed up inside of
the school. The teacher for the television series would
provide the student with food. The parents of this child were
addicted to drugs, and their addiction had taken over their
lives.

My question is: Does this define a good teacher? Should
all teachers draw outside of these lines? The answer is both
yes than no. Yes, the teacher was being the difference in that
child's life, and helping him with issues that were affecting

him inside of the classroom, but what happens when the
child moves from one grade level to the next? What happens
when the teacher could no longer wash the student's clothes,
or provide him with a meal each day? Another question is
what happens when there are at least ten students going
through the same exact challenges that this student faced?

When a teacher decides to draw outside of the lines, he
or she must make sure that they stay within some perimeters
and never overstep their boundaries, or make a situation
worse in the long-term. This is one of the reasons why a
parent should be encouraged to participate in school
activities. Believe me when I say that most parents truly want
to be a part of their children's educational journey. A caring
teacher might need to show them how to do that.

The question still remains, what defines a good teacher? I
believe the following qualities define a great teacher:

- Empathy

- Patience

- Flexibility

- and a Sense of Humor

The days can be stressful for both teacher and students, which is why having a sense of humor, along with patience is great. The lives of the students can be just as challenging at home, as the task of teaching each student inside of the classroom is for the teachers, which is why empathy is an important quality. Again, what the teacher in the HBO television series did for that one student was great, but the question still remains, did he actually help the student, or make it worse? This is a question that new and veteran teachers within the school system will have to answer each year. As more students enter my classroom each year, I feel their challenges every day. I want to help them with the issues they have at home, and I want to help them excel as a student in the classroom. However, it is my duty to work effectively with a wide-range of children who come from different backgrounds. I have to show strong leadership each

day; it is my job as a teacher to motivate students to learn.
That is what defines a great teacher.

As a new teacher, I struggled with knowing what could
help my students learn. I wanted them to find their own
"Candy Land," but that was a challenge I endured the
moment my first set of students walked through my
classroom door. Many of the students did not have a lot of
respect for me, but it was my job to respect them, regardless
of their backgrounds. I had to make them believe that they
could learn; it was my job to motivate them to learn, and it
was my duty to help them understand that they were capable
of learning and succeeding in life. A teacher in urban schools
will have the challenge of making each student believe that
they have a right to a bright future. Accepting that challenge
was my job, and helping my students believe in themselves is
what makes me a great teacher. Is it difficult to do? Yes! Can
it be done? Yes!

How could I get through to students in school, when
they were dealing with the difficult issues that they faced at

home? This is where drawing outside of the classroom comes into play. Now I could not be the "parent" for each child, but I could be their teacher. Having parent-teacher conferences is something that every school district does, but when the parents refuse to show up for the child, there is pretty much nothing the teacher can do. This is when an educator needs to draw outside of the lines.

Students in poor school districts are likely to have more inexperienced teachers compared to veteran educators. However, this does not mean a student should be given less education; it does not give teachers an excuse not to teach accordingly. While I did not have the experience that a veteran teacher had, I did have the credentials. I was taught the fundamentals to become an effective teacher, but it was my job to take what I had learned and make it work for the benefit of my students. Going back to my social studies class… Every teacher does not teach the same way, and not all of my teachers allowed me to create a country and have fun with a subject or topic like that; however, every teacher did have their own unique method to help students learn.

That is what being a great teacher is all about. Take the
student and teacher from the television series *The Wire*; what
would benefit the student if he was only offered clean clothes
and food, but no education? Teachers have to prepare
students for what awaits them in life. One day our students
move on to another grade level, and they must be ready to
learn at every level in order receive their high school diploma
– and hopefully a college degree.

My social studies teacher took the right approach with
me, and suddenly a boring class became not so boring. I was
already the student who was eager to learn, but that moment
made me the student that loved to learn. It made me the
student who wanted to learn so much that I could eventually
become the teacher, which is exactly what I did. So even
when faced with challenges inside of the classroom, I decided
to learn what would motivate my students to learn. Just like
businesses must keep up with the current trends, a teacher
should as well. New teachers and veterans alike must come
into the classroom wanting to teach a child, wanting to help
the child, and drawing outside of the classroom lines to make

sure that each child knows they have a bright future ahead of themselves. This will require a teacher to be great, and know the children that are behind the desks…

CHAPTER 3:

THE CHILDREN BEHIND THE DESKS

"A good teacher must be able to put himself in the place of those who find learning hard." - Eliphas Levi

From the moment that I stepped foot into my classroom, I knew that I had an important job to do. Teaching my students the importance of an education was my job, and I was determined to do it. I could not be one of those teachers who accepted defeat before I actually faced the opponent. The children in my classroom were not opponents, they were my students. They were here to learn, and I was here to teach them.

I believe the appearance of the classroom was one of the reasons why I thought meeting my students would be a difficult task. I had not expected to walk into what I had that morning, so I was preparing myself for what could be next:

the worse. However, no matter how many times I told myself what my class would be like, but the fact was that I had no idea. You cannot actually prepare yourself for that first meeting with your students, regardless of how many years you teach. Times change, and children change. This is one of the reasons why I mentioned teachers need to change with the times in the previous chapter. I could use the same approach year after year, but the students would be different each time. But let's get back to this time, and this particular group of students...

This experience was truly amazing. As each student filled the classroom, I felt myself reliving that moment when I realized I wanted to be a teacher. Even with the lack of acknowledgement that I was there by other teachers and administrators, I was happy. As the years go by, and I help draw outside of the lines, but I never receive the acknowledgement from other teachers that I deserve, meeting my class always takes me back to that happy place. I am reminded why I wanted to teach, and when I face a challenge with my students, I remember how I felt the day they first walked through my door. It is like being in the backyard teaching all over again. Now, some of the children are not eager to learn like those fourth-graders in my childhood were, but teaching is still something that I would do over and over again… It is truly an indescribable feeling.

As Ramon walked into my classroom, I noticed he was wearing a baseball cap. Some people believe a person wears a baseball cap to be attractive, or to cover up the fact that they are going bald. I believe Ramon was wearing his cap to be "cool." It was the current trend, and had I not been up-to-date with trends, I might have thought he was trying to cover up the fact that his hair had not been combed, instead of wanting to be considered "cool." His hair was black in color, and kinky in texture; I later learned that the kinky look was "in" at the moment. I wanted to learn more about Ramon, just from the first encounter. He greeted me by saying, "What up folk!"

The next student to enter the classroom was Nyea. I wish I could say that she was as happy and outgoing as Ramon had been, but she was not. In fact, I was under the impression that she wanted to fight me. Honestly, she walked by me and growled as she looked me up and down, from head-to-toe. This was definitely not in the educational psychology books that I had read in college. Did she want to fight me? What would I do if she did? In my mind, I kept remembering that this was Candy Land, and I had to be the difference, even with Nyea. Later on, I was informed that Nyea had "mean mugged" me, which means that she gave me a distasteful facial expression that matched how she felt at that moment.

TJ was the next student to grace my classroom, and his greeting was a little friendlier. Even though he did not give me any startling stares, I knew instantly that he would be the "class clown." He was extremely polite, but I was not fooled by his "polite" behavior. He said, "How you do today, Ms. Teacher?" His devious smile is what stood out the most. Yes, I would have my hands full with TJ, as well as all of the "TJs" that were sure to follow me throughout my teaching career.

TJ helped ease the tension of me being a new teacher,
and the tension my students had adapting to a new teacher.
He positioned himself in the middle of the classroom, and
performed a nerdy/geeky type of dance move, while
snapping his fingers and moving from side-to-side. The
entire class was laughing, and I even caught myself bursting
with laughter as well. The mood had instantly changed, all
because I chose to have a sense of humor. You see, I could
never truly get to know my students if I did not allow them
to be themselves. Some new teachers believe you have to
teach each student military style, but that is not my motto. I
want children to be free in my classroom, because when they
are free, their minds are open freely to learn.

As TJ was doing his dance, I noticed that the clothes on
this 11-year-old student were way too big for him. I was not
sure if this was a choice, or if it was his only option. It was
my job to know, so that I could teach him better. I had to
remember that I was not there to be his parent or best-friend,
but I was there to make a difference. So finding out the

challenges he had at home would help me teach him better
inside of the classroom.

Portia's clothes were the complete opposite of TJ's; her
jeans were skin-tight. I had no idea how she managed to walk
comfortably with those jeans on, but she did. Portia sashayed
passed me to her desk, without saying hello. She had on fake
nails, along with braids that were long, thick, and down her
back. For a child in the sixth grade, she was well-developed.
She was extremely comfortable with her development, and
she loved the attention her shape earned her when she
walked into the classroom.

The student, that to this day, sticks out to me the most
was Brandee. She was thirteen years of age – older than the
other sixth graders. Her age is not what captured my
attention; it was the fact that she was pregnant. This child
had the sweetest and cutest face; her face was truly childlike,
yet here she was about to have a child. Given the size of her
stomach, I would say she would have that child sooner,
rather than later. I looked forward to teaching this

nonchalant student for the remainder of the year. I wanted to be the difference in her life, but that chance was taken away from me when Brandee was removed from my class before the end of the school year. We had some wonderful, "breakthrough" moments during her brief time as my student. My only hope is that she received the education that she needed to be the difference in her child's life.

Brina is the student that every teacher loves… She was prepared. When Brina walked into my class, she had her notebook in hand, along with some folders, and several pencils. She was a plump girl in size, and her skin complexion was a smooth, chocolate. She had a head full of ponytails with barrettes that matched her outfit. Brina was a true sixth grade student, in comparison to Brandee. I wondered why she was able to live life as a child, and why Brandee had decided to take another approach in life. Was it by choice?

Another student who matched my idea of what the sixth grade student would be like was Sophie. She was a very thin girl who wore big, framed glasses. She had a short afro

hairstyle, and her skin was a silky, caramel color. Sophie, just
like Brina, was youthful, full of innocence, and eager to learn.

Brina and Sophie were similar to the children that I
taught in my backyard during my youth. It was at that
moment that I realized, every experience would not be like
that, and every child would not live up to this pre-conceived
notion that I, along with countless teachers, have. Did this
mean that children who were different deserved to receive a
different education? Should they be treated any less than a
child who fit the typical good student description? NO! This
is why so many educators turn down teaching jobs in urban
school districts; they do not want to take on the task of
helping students who possess the most challenges. When the
truth is, students like Brandee and Nyea are just as eager to
learn, they just have more obstacles to overcome in order to
get to the point where they want to learn. But that was my
job; my duty. I was the social studies teacher, and they were
me. It was my duty to help them come out of their bored
mind-frame and have that epitome… I had to help them
realize that learning was fun!

In order to get my students to learn, I had to break down the walls that were currently separating us. It was my job to get-to-know the students behind the desk in my class. Do not be under the misconception that you only have to do this once, and then you become a professional. While teachers do develop methods that work best to learn their students; the fact remains that even veteran teachers have to change up their teaching style sometimes, in order to keep up with the new trends.

Preparing teachers to work in urban schools is something that many educational systems have struggled with in the past, but today, more and more schools are better preparing teachers for their future classrooms in urban schools. Each year, student populations in urban schools become more diverse, and the classrooms become more complex. Educational institutions are realizing that teachers need more than a general education; educators also need knowledge of the learning styles and lives pertaining to the inner city students that they will teach. This is why many school districts in non-suburban areas have begun to improve their teacher induction programs, in order to address the needs of both the students and teachers in inner city schools. The challenge for new teachers entering school systems that lack funding and resources remains an issue as well, but this is an issue that many school districts are trying to change for the better.

The Atlanta Public School System had one of the most publicized criminal cases in educational history. The teachers and administrators in this school district were changing the test answers of students in order to help them pass from one grade level to another. This is in no way legal, nor should it be condoned. The children lose out, and the teacher does too. The teachers involved were cheating for many reasons; some were paid to do it, others were doing so to truly do what they felt would benefit the students, and some cheated out of fear of being fired.

The fact remains that cheating is never a good thing to do, regardless of grade level. Cheating distracts a student from learning, and reaching his true potential. Cheating also builds bad habits that follow children into their adult lives, such as stealing, slacking in their professional careers, and looking for the easy way out in most situations. Instead of cheating, the APS officials should have devoted more time to helping the students learn. Similar to the student in The Wire, what happens when the students move on to the next grade level? How will they function when they have not learned? The teachers who encourage cheating are helping a student learn to fail, instead of motivating the student to learn and succeed.

It is true that a student's lack of educational success can be attributed to the financial and social disadvantages that students in low-income communities have. Many researchers and philosophers blame the people living inside of these disadvantaged communities for the failure, claiming that if the people want to live better, they need to move. Sadly, it is not that black and white in this society. In order to move into affluent neighborhoods with stellar school systems, families need the funds and resources. There is no sense in moving from one low-income community to another; this does not solve the main issue.

Society often deems children in low-income communities as failures before they have had a chance to succeed. This is one of the reasons why students in urban school districts do not receive the funds for necessary resources. Studies have shown that the third-grade reading level will predict if a prison bed is built for a student in a low-income community. Instead of spending that money to prepare children for a bright, successful future, the funds are being spent to build prisons that will house the students one day. While this is one of the many reasons why every educator in an urban school district should want to work that much harder to help their students, it is in no way a reason why teachers should cheat – or teach children to cheat.

When I signed up to teach in an urban school, I was not prepared for what met me at the door. I was not prepared for how I was supposed to teach my students, and I was not prepared on how I could motivate them to be successful. I was thinking that every student would be like Brina and Sophie; therefore, I was not prepared when I was assigned to a classroom to teach Brandee, TJ, and Nyea. That was not my fault, and it definitely was not the fault of the students. What new teachers in urban school systems need to know is that they must embrace a process that consist of constructing and reconstructing in practice; the purpose of this is to help create an approach that provides students with meaningful and productive learning experiences.

The pre-packaged program instruction new teachers receive rarely, if ever, meets the needs of students attending urban schools. This is why teachers need to get-to-know the students behind each of the desks that are filled in the classroom. It is necessary to create a process that allows teachers to develop approaches that are carefully crafted and designed to meet the educational learning levels of each student. A teacher in urban schools will need to know more than just a student's name; they will need to know what the student values, what they know, and what they have yet to learn. It is the responsibility of the teacher to know the

experiences of each student inside of the classroom, as well
as outside of the classroom. A teacher is not a parent or best-
friend, but they are the difference, and sometimes that
requires more than teaching, it requires a teacher to know the
student behind the desk.

My students looked like me, as far as race, but they were
nothing like me. They were not like the students that I taught
in my backyard, and they were not like the students that
college had prepared me to teach; however, it was my duty to
provide them with a great education. I had the duty of
motivating each student to work hard in order to achieve a
better future. It was my desire to help the children create
their very own Candy Land. I would not achieve this by
teaching them how to cheat; I needed to create linkages to
the student's current learning experiences, and develop a way
to build upon that. My curriculum would need to extend
beyond the traditional curriculum. It would need to coincide
with the experiences, realities, and the identities of the
students who sat behind the desks in my classrooms, which is
why I needed to learn them.

Every student was different, yet they all deserved a dedicated teacher who would respect them, understand them, teach them, motivate them, and believe in them. Turning ones back on students should never be the practice of any educator, in any school system. I now had a chance to make a difference, and that is exactly what I was going to do. College does not always prepare you to be the difference; but it is your duty to learn how to be one. That is what defines a good teacher, which is why all teachers in urban schools need to learn more about applying diversity inside of modern classrooms...

CHAPTER 4:

DIVERSITY INSIDE OF THE MODERN CLASSROOM

*"The object of education is to prepare the young to educate themselves throughout
their lives." – Robert M. Hutchins*

The United States continues to become a diverse country; the
term melting-pot fits the classroom more and more each
year, and the same is true within most of the walls of
classrooms throughout the U.S. This is one of the reasons
why the classroom must be made into a place where students
can strive to be great. Each child deserves to learn so that
they can secure a bright future for themselves. The struggle
with many teachers in the modern classroom is teaching to a
diverse group of students. As the demographics continue to
change in schools each year, teachers will need to change
their classroom learning techniques in order to accommodate
their students.

The first step toward providing students with a multicultural education is understanding what that means. Does it mean throwing a party on May 5th of each year for students of Spanish origin? Perhaps it is reading a book in January about the late, great Dr. Martin Luther King, Jr. The answer is none of the above. Instead, the lessons should be centered around an educational movement that is built on the basic American values that exist in today's culture, which include equality, freedom, justice, and opportunity. The educational strategy of the classroom should be aimed toward the challenges that all people within the country are experiencing. After all, the demographics in the United States continue to change, rapidly.

I learned early on that just like I wanted my students to create goals, I too would need to create some goals of my own. When the children walked into my classroom, they needed me to provide them with an educational plan that would work for them. It is my duty as an educator to ensure that the students are truly learning. When students of various racial backgrounds come into my class each year, I make it

my main goal to provide them all with a multicultural
education. Some of the goals that I create for myself are to
ensure that I am providing each and every student with:

- A safe, accepting, and successful learning environment

- An increasing amount of awareness in regards to
global issues

- Strengthening cultural consciousness

- Educational lessons that stress the multiple historical
perspectives

- Encouragement toward critical thinking

- Knowledge that prevents prejudice and discrimination

Despite what many philosophers may believe, there are a
great deal of advantages associated with a multicultural
education, especially when it is taught inside of a diverse
classroom. When the children in my classrooms receive a
quality, multicultural education, they are able to develop a

positive self-image, which is something that I believe is
extremely important. So many children see themselves in a
negative light, and that is something that teachers need to
help change. Each student has the capability of being great,
and teachers must help them see the greatness that is there.
Often students in urban schools have issues realizing their
true potential, due to their current circumstances. While this
is not true for each student, I have noticed it with many of
the children that walk through the doors of my classroom
each year. Each child is different, but that is what makes
them so great. The world is full of different racial groups and
ethnicities, yet that is a positive that makes our country so
great. Regardless of a student's nationality, or income
bracket, they all deserve a chance to excel, and it is a teacher's
responsibility to make sure they have a positive self-image,
especially when they may not receive that type of positive
influence inside of their home or within their community.

Teachers should offer their students an equitable
educational opportunity. I learned early on that I needed to
allow multiple perspectives and ways of thinking inside of my

classroom. I remember teaching my class on that first day, and I have to admit, I was not prepared. I had a lesson plan ready to go, but it was not a plan that should be used for every group of children. In college, students learn about teaching guides that will help them inside of the classroom, but sometimes teachers need to change these guides, and their teaching practices, in order to meet the needs of each student. Curriculum guides were created in order to provide a framework for quality content, but these guides were never meant to replace the help that students give teachers when designing relevant lesson plans and teaching techniques. Educators that use a "one-size fits all" type of teaching design are sure to fail when it pertains to meeting the needs of their students.

The first lesson I provided on my first day was English. Remember that I came in the middle of the school year, so I had to pick up right where the previous teacher had left off. My students were learning about comparing and contrasting at that moment, and I was ready to use my teacher's guide – it had become my crutch. I pulled out ditto sheets and the students worked on worksheets. I felt that was the safest way to teach. Regardless of what set of students were in front of me, this was the curriculum that I was going to go with. However, every day I watched students struggle with the lesson. I saw my class become disconnected with this teaching style each day. They were bored, and they had no desire to learn. I watched them slip further away from developing their own Candy Land, and I knew that I had to do something. I was teaching a diverse set of students, which meant that traditional teaching techniques would not work with this group of children. I needed to provide a more diverse learning style for my students.

After thinking about how I could not only make learning interesting, I thought about how I could connect with each student in my classroom. I wanted them to have the moment I experienced in my younger days. I knew that in order for my students to have their own epitomes, I would have to design a teaching strategy that suited them. The guide that became my crutch was still valuable, but my teaching style needed to change so that it would be culturally relevant. Each

year, the group of students inside of the classroom will not
only change, but the teaching trends for that year will change
as well. Teachers will need to get to know each of their
students, and make teaching choices accordingly.

The day that I decided to try something different was a
great day for my students. As they walked into the classroom,
I had drawn two circles on the chalkboard. The circles had
overlapped – I now know that this is referred to as a Venn
Diagram. Inside of one circle, I had the name MLK Jr. Inside
of the other circle were the words Gang Leader. I noticed the
look of surprise and curiosity as each student entered the
room that day. I had not only shocked them with my
teaching approach, but I had piqued their interest. I was
talking amongst myself as I waited for each student to enter
the classroom. Even though I was speaking directly to
myself, I made sure my voice was loud enough for the
students to hear me. I was saying things like, "Oh, MLK was
basically a gang leader." I used MLK because it was the day
before his birthday. The students were looking at me as if I
had lost my mind, and the fact that I had made them open

their minds was great. One student asked me, "What are you doing?" That was the start of our classroom discussion. I decided to play obtuse, in regards to what defined a gang leader. The students began teaching me the characteristics of a gang leader, and what made that type of person similar, as well as different, from MLK.

Each student had begun taking notes, and I asked them to use those notes for our next writing piece. Their assignment was to write about MLK Jr., and tell me what type of man he was, and how he would speak with a gang leader if he was able to come back to Earth for just one day. I still remember my excitement as I read each of the writing pieces; they were amazing! The grammar for some of the papers was not its best, but we could work on that. The most amazing thing to come from this lesson was the content of each paper. I had helped my students use critical thinking, which I touched on previously in this chapter. My job is to help push the students to think critically, and that is exactly what I had done. I did this by changing the teacher's guide that I had held on to tightly during my first couple of days as a new teacher. When I decided to relate the curriculum guide to my students, they became interested with the lesson. The students felt like I had in my social studies class over a decade ago – Learning was fun! My students became interested in their own Candy Land, and it started with me allowing a different learning perspective for my students. I allowed a different way of thinking, and it worked. This is another way that teachers can understand and get to know the children that are behind the desk.

When teaching a group of students from the same background, it is the job of the teacher to ensure multicultural learning still takes place. Preparing a student for a bright future in a modern society requires more than learning about one's culture. The world is a melting pot, and students should learn the skills to not only adapt with that melting pot, but the skills that are necessary to thrive in it as well.

Even though my students were predominantly black, they still had different backgrounds. Some of my students came from two-parent homes, while others lived in single-parent homes. My class consisted of students from low-income families, as well as children living in middle class homes. A majority of the students were encouraged by their families to come to school and receive a great education, but unfortunately, some students did not receive that same type of push at home.

Social class is not the only characteristic that made my class diverse. Complexion also played a factor with some of my students. Since the days of "passing," individuals with a lighter complexion are often seen as more acceptable than people who have a darker skin color. I believe every child deserves to learn, regardless of complexion; however, this was another barrier that I would need to help my students break down. Outside of color, religion also played an important role in how some of my students viewed themselves. I remember one of my students, Paula, wore skirts instead of pants; something that her religion did not allow. Another student of mine, Georgia, wore head scarves and floor length skirts, a culture learned through her Muslim faith. It was not my job to divide the students; instead, it was my job to teach them all how to learn and accept the cultures of their peers. Children cannot understand what they do not know, which is why they are inside of the classroom – they are there to learn. In a diverse classroom, students learn more than what the textbook has outlined. My students learned about various cultures, and the people within them. My students would study with a diverse set of children, and in adulthood, they would work in the same career fields as the people who make up the melting pot that is America. This is another reason why it was important to teach diversity within a modern classroom.

It is a myth that teachers do all of the teaching inside of the classroom. The truth is that students teach educators as well. Many teachers will encounter diverse cultures, just like the students. Teachers must go on a journey to uncover how different cultures influence families, as well as the language of people and where they live. Teachers need to be prepared to make the bold changes inside of their classrooms that allow each student to feel included in the classroom discussions. As teachers change their teaching styles to incorporate a broader view of the world, they will learn as well.

Many educators do not know where to begin. The truth is that there is no wrong or right place to begin. I started with the MLK scenario, but other teachers can dive right into various cultures. For instance, a teacher could discuss the communities where various immigrants once lived, including those immigrants that are African American, Chinese, and Russian. Students will be able to find the similarities and differences between these cultures and their own cultures.

It is also a good idea to invite guest speakers into the classroom who have diverse backgrounds. Bringing guest speakers into the classroom is not only a great way to introduce students to professions and career choices, but it allows students the opportunity to reflect on what they could become. Choose from colleagues or community professionals such as bankers, dentists, police officers, nurses, politicians, doctors, store owners, and more. Be sure to choose guests speakers who are not only diverse, but individuals that represent diverse professions as well. These presentations can also help students relate what they are studying to their own lives.

Teachers that are sensitive to cultural differences could be of tremendous value to the classroom. This is something that the traditional teacher's guide does not have listed, but you will need to know it as you help teach diversity inside of a modern classroom.

Teachers need to look at their classroom and decide if they are making the lessons relatable to each student. Is the curriculum something that the students can actively engage in and learn at the same time? Does this help students learn more about their culture, as well as the cultures of others?

Sometimes teachers believe that just because they are the same color as students, they automatically know each student. This is not true! I was the same shade of color as the majority of my students; however, we were not the same. The teaching staff for the students within my school was not diverse. Yet, I had made it my goal to create a transformative curriculum, and design a learning community that reflected a multicultural society. I wanted to help the students who did not feel like they fit in. I wanted each child to know that they were more, and that they deserved more.

CHAPTER 5:

CHARACTERISTICS AND COLORS

"Preservation of one's own culture does not require contempt or disrespect for other cultures." - Cesar Chavez

When I was a student, I wanted to learn, and the more I learned, the more I wanted to learn. I learned everything pertaining to my culture, as well as the cultures of others around me. This is something that I feel all schools should offer, and all new teachers should become accustomed with. Providing real learning opportunities to students should be the main focus of teachers, regardless if the children share the same cultural backgrounds as other students or school staff.

Many schools have this "mismatch" learning environment. I was one of the four black teachers in a predominantly black school. There were twenty staff members in total: three were black females, one black male, five white males, and eleven white females. In addition to being the newest staff member at my school, I was also the youngest. Many people had high hopes for me, as a new teacher. They expected me to come into the classroom and save the day. I remember Mr. Moore, one of the security aides at the school. He patted me on the back as he passed by me in the hallway. He leaned over, looking at me with a big grin on his face, and he whispered into my ear, "We are glad to have a black teacher. That class of yours is out of control!"

It is true that any class can be full of students who talk while their teacher is lecturing, or sleep when they should be learning. It does not matter what color a group of students are, being out-of-control is a characteristic that an entire class can have based on actions, not skin color. I remember that I was not interested in learning until my teachers would make the lesson fun, so at times, I became disengaged. This in no way meant I was uncontrollable.

Once the class began, it felt like the worst day of my life. The students did not want me there, and I began to question if I wanted to be there. I did not know if I was ready to be a teacher, especially on this teaching assignment. I began to think about all of the reasons why I had accepted this teaching assignment, and all I could come up with was the fact that it had been assigned. When people warned me against accepting an assignment in an urban school, I would respond by saying how I too was black; therefore, I would not have a difficult time teaching my students.

Some of my students had the same skin complexion that I had; however, we were extremely different. I became aware of how different my students and I were when the children began to fill the classroom one-by-one. Some of the students were nice like TJ, helping me melt the ice, but some of the students were similar to Neya, and they could care less about me being there.

Gone were my thoughts about being a black teacher in an urban school. I had this vision of what it would be like, and quite naturally I imagined that I would soar because I had something in common with my students. That is where I failed before even stepping foot inside of the classroom, and new teachers should avoid this type of thinking as well. There is nothing magical about being black in an urban school, just like there is nothing magical about being a white teacher in an all-white school.

If there were special powers associated with being black and teaching in an urban school, I would have loved to use them, especially on my first day. The kids did not relate to me, but I would quickly learn that was because I did not relate to the kids. This goes back to not truly knowing what it meant to be in a diverse classroom. While diversity can be about race, that is not all. Diversity defines people coming together from different races, religions, sexes, and nationalities. Diversity also pertains to some organizations, groups, and communities. What I learned through teaching is the true meaning of diversity: an organization or individual that values the difference within other people.

So here I was a black teacher, with a class that was predominantly black, but my main objectives as a teacher was to motivate each student to think critically. Well, diversity is a sure way to create curiosity. Students who are exposed to different cultures and backgrounds want to learn more about those individuals. One group of people could give another group insight into the culture and how things are done. This is a positive for teachers because it helps students begin to search for other ways to help change their lives for the better.

Diverse schools prepare students for bright futures. Students learn how to prepare for the real world through education, and through diversity. Students who can take a stand on a subject could potentially voice their own opinion on the subject as they continue through school, and into their adult life. It is true that one person cannot get something done for the community or a business, but a group of diverse talents can be strength in numbers.

I know that the students in my first school would have liked to see more teachers that were similar to their skin

complexion, but that does not define diversity. Students
operate better within the real world when they receive a
quality education from a diverse setting. The students not
only have a better view of life, but they will receive a better
understanding as well.

A teacher never knows what to expect when walking into
a classroom of students; however, a teacher should never
expect each child to be same. While some of my students
were the same skin complexion as me, we could not have
been further opposites. I find that more fascinating as ever.
As I have said in the previous chapter, students do a little bit
of teaching in the classroom as well. My students taught me
the various experiences that someone with the same skin
complexion as me has encountered. My students also taught
me that even with their harsh realities and circumstances,
they wanted to try and change their lives for the better. That
right there makes teaching well worth the hard work,
dedication, and commitment...

When I think about Mr. Moore patting me on the back, I hear the negative way in which he spoke about the children in my classroom. These were children that I learned to care about, and children who have left great impressions with me over the years.

It is important for teachers to embrace the cultures of each student in their class. Their students will feel important when they take the time to get to know them, instead of referring to them as uncontrollable students. A diverse classroom opened the door to many great things, and the students feeling as if they belonged was one. Students learning in a more diverse environment are less likely to shut others out. Instead, they learn more about others, which helps every student fit in.

Diversity is – and will continue to be – more helpful to the classroom than harmful. The differences between the students within a class help to improve people. When teachers learn to celebrate the differences that the students have, they can work to help transform their classrooms, as well as the communities that these urban schools are placed within.

I think back to the students I taught in my backyard… They were not similar, but they all wanted to learn. I had to take what I was taught in school, and apply it in a way that they would understand. The same scenario applies today, but the children are older, and I am a certified educator. The fact remains that every child deserves his or her own Candy Land, regardless of race, social status, ethnicity, gender, or religion.

CHAPTER 6:

HELPING STUDENTS BEYOND THE CURRICULUM

"Failure to prepare is preparing to fail." – Mike Murdock

As a new teacher, I knew that it was my job to teach students the curriculum for their grade level, but I never thought about what my job was outside of teaching. Learning about each student behind the desks was something I took upon myself, and helping students face their realities was something that I knew I would have to take on as well. Children do not ask to be born into poverty, or areas where the crime rate is higher than a graduation rate. However, this is often the reality of the diverse set of students that walk through my classroom doors, as well as countless classrooms around the world.

The violence that follows students around is often due to no fault of their own, yet they still carry this burden, which often spills over into the classroom. While I was in college, I never learned about a student being placed on probation, especially students at the elementary school level. Since I did not learn about this aspect of the classroom, I was extremely shocked when I had a student in this very predicament. Likewise, I was not prepared to teach students who were forced to witness a horrific crime one night, and be a great student the very next day. Yet I experienced this all within my first year as a new teacher in an urban school.

I tried an experiment in class one day; I allowed my students to discuss current events. I wanted to know what was going on in their lives, and what they felt was important at that moment. This was my attempt to bring the real world into the classroom. After all, it was my job to prepare each student for the realities outside of the classroom. What I experienced next was something I did not expect. I was not prepared when one of my students, Philip, told me that his

uncle had been gunned down and killed right down the street
from their home.

I was floored when Philip described the awful event.
However, I think what shocked me the most was the manner
in which Philip told his story. He described his uncle being
shot and murdered before his own eyes, just like he would
have described a basketball game that he had watched on
television the night before. Some of the students in the
classroom responded by saying, "For real?" or "That's sad."
Other students began sharing similar stories that they had
experienced in the past. It was at that moment that I wanted
to comfort each of the children in my classroom. College had
not prepared me for this. I was told – by my students – that
this type of situation occurs all of the time; it was the "norm"
for their community.

The children told me how they had to make "safe
choices" in the community, so that they could avoid being
victims of these types of incidents. As I listened to the
students talk, I realized we would fall behind schedule, and I

would not be able to keep up with the lesson. However, in this instance, my students were more important than the curriculum. They were venting about their lives, and it was my job to listen. My students were not discussing the latest technologies, or the current fashion trends; instead, they were discussing how they could avoid being gunned down in their neighborhoods.

I decided to allow my students to channel their energy in a positive way. I wanted them to feel richer from learning something, and that day it was to speak with someone who could provide them with scenarios that would work outside of the classroom. I encouraged them to do great in school so that they could earn scholarships for college. I told my students that earning a college degree would allow them to apply for well-paying jobs that could help them provide for their families. School was their outlet, and the students needed to know that they could accomplish anything. It was my job to help them realize that with hard work, motivation, and dedication, the sky was truly the limit.

I wish I could say that every year, things get better, but that is not true. Many students living in low-income communities experience horrific killings and situations on a daily basis. This type of trauma could wreak havoc on a child's learning ability. It is a fact that children who repetitively experience the type of trauma that Philip and his peers had suffered from lead to social, biological, cognitive, and psychological issues. It is often difficult for them to pay attention in class; they also have a hard time regulating their emotions; and it is extremely difficult for the students to form positive relationships.

What students do learn about during college is bullying. It is almost impossible to log onto the internet or turn on the television and not see a news report pertaining to bullying, or see an advertisement urging the world to come together to stop school bullying. I knew all about bullying, because it is something that many people experience or witness in their own childhood. However, here I was face-to-face with bullying within the school walls, and I was no longer a child, but the adult. It was my responsibility to help my students realize the harsh realities that pertained to bullying, and how they should handle the situation should it happen to them.

I recall one horrible bullying situation that took place at school during my first year as a new teacher. Although the bullying did not take place inside of my classroom, it affected my students just the same. In this specific instance, a group of three students had been arrested for attacking another student. They had beat him up, and stolen his personal property. I remember hearing the details, and thinking about how serious this situation was for the student who had been attacked, as well as the students who were responsible for the actual attack.

The three students had summonsed the student, claiming that they needed to ask him a question. Once the student was within their reach, one student knocked him down, began to beat him, and pulled out a firearm to threaten the student. The attacker went on to steal the student's jacket. The aftermath was a student left in critical condition, and three other students being arrested for committing the crime. It

was a senseless matter that no teacher is prepared to handle,
but it happens.

These were not three strangers; these were students who
all knew each other. They were all students within the same
school, and saw each other on a weekly basis. When I think
about the students, I could not help but to feel sorry for all
of them. As a teacher, it is impossible to know what is going
through a child's mind, but it is our job to try and find out.
Yes, educators must teach the curriculum given to them, but
teachers must also help their students deal with the harsh
realities that impact them inside and outside of the
classroom.

Now a new teacher may be wondering how these
situations are relevant to teaching curriculum, and the answer
is, extremely! Most teachers believe that teaching curriculum
is all that is required of them. While this may be true, a
teacher should also go beyond the curriculum and learn
about the student behind the desk. Getting to know that
student means that a teacher goes beyond the traditional

teaching requirements, which is necessary when teachers want to help their students prepare for the realities outside of the classroom.

I could have allowed the bullying incident to go by without discussing it with my students. I could have ignored the fact that a student of mine was on parole. Or I could be like countless other teachers who hope that the harsh realities our students deal with in their homes and communities do not come inside the classroom. Well, the truth is that those realities do come inside of the classroom, and in most cases, they can impact every student. I wanted to be more than the teacher that teaches; I wanted to be the teacher that cared. After all, great teachers do more than teach – they make a difference.

In order for me to make a difference, I had to go beyond what the curriculum stated. I remember one of my students named Romelo was on parole. As a new teacher, this was shocking. I had never read about this, and if I had, it still would have shocked me when I learned I had to give a report

to the student's counselor, his parent, and his parole officer
on a regular basis. Romelo had been involved in committing
a crime. I never learned the full details, and what I did know
came from fellow students and teachers.

Apparently, Romelo had been involved in a robbery. He
was with his older cousins when they attempted to rob a local
gas station. Even with a crime as serious as that, I saw
Romelo as a good student and child. On the outside, he
looked like a rough kid in appearance. One would think he
was much older than a sixth grader, but he was not. When I
talked with him, I saw that he was a good kid on the inside.
When we had our one-on-one discussions, he was the
sweetest child that I had ever met. Even though I did not
have much time to work with him, I knew that the outside
world was affecting him inside of the classroom.

Romelo never cursed at me, but I had heard him curse at
other teachers. Once, he cursed out another teacher when
she drilled him about coming to class unprepared, and
unmotivated. That earned him a suspension, and

unfortunately, Romelo never returned to school. This specific incident symbolized how some teachers feel that curriculum is more important than a student.

We were there to make a difference in Romelo's life, like someone had made in ours. In this case, Romelo was suspended, and he chose not to return to school. I often wonder what happened to Romelo, and if he continued on a path that would lead to greatness, or if he took the destructive path. A lot of children need that extra push, and unfortunately, not enough teachers are willing to provide that nudge. Teachers have a duty of being a difference, and that extends beyond the state approved curriculum.

I stand by my statement that teachers do not need to be the parent, but they do need to be the teacher who cares. As I sat with Romelo, he was nothing like the reputation he had gained from other students and teachers. Instead, he was a sweet child who made mistakes. Those mistakes could have been corrected with a little bit of guidance. When teachers fail to help their students do better academically and sociably, they are failing the students. Statistics show that one out of every three African American boys will end up imprisoned within their lifetime. One in six Latino males will end up in jail at least once within their lifetime. This number is unacceptable, especially when teachers have the potential to do something to prevent it.

Children are not born criminals, nor do they aspire to be suspended from school. Some of the students I have had over the years hide behind masks, afraid that if they do not curse out teachers, threaten their peers, or participate in criminal activity, they could be the victim of bullying or worse. It is a teacher's job to help students realize that violence is never the way. Teachers can do so by taking the extra time to help students after school by conducting after-school programs, or community organized events. Getting the parents more involved with their children is one of the goals that these programs could provide.

When children struggle to rely on their parents for safety, it makes it almost impossible for them to trust anyone, even teachers. This is why teachers must know the signs. When children lash out, teachers must respond with compassion. These children are in survival mode, and educators must respond in a gentle way, giving the student choices. For instance, when Romelo lashed out at his teachers, the educators should have responded with choices. "You seem like you are getting irritated, so what can we do to ease the situation?" Or a teacher could respond with, "I see you are having trouble with this problem, this is what we can do to fix it."

When a teacher creates a calm, predictable transition, they can eliminate the activities that cause triggers, which lead to a student going into survival mode. Playing music or ringing a meditation bell often helps.

I remember thinking as a new teacher that I would rather be writing a recommendation for my student's scholarship application, instead of the letter of character that could reduce his probation sentence. It brought tears to my eyes when a parent asked me for the latter, and that is one of the moments when I realized that curriculum is never more important than the student. I am glad that my social studies teacher decided to go away from the traditional curriculum-teaching techniques. I was given the chance to create something that gave me a whole new perspective on life – my very own Candy Land. Each child deserves that, and it is up to teachers to help students realize their true potential. Teachers must help beyond the curriculum, or they too are failing their students.

Chapter 7:

Owning Your Lesson Plans

"A good teacher, like a good entertainer first must hold his audience's attention, then he can teach his lesson." – John Henrik Clarke

Effective teaching and learning begins with good lesson planning. Teachers that are well prepared have a better chance at achieving a successful instructional experience. When it pertains to developing a lesson plan, this should be something that all new and veteran teachers devote a great deal of time and thought to. Even though it is a time-consuming process, all teachers should be committed to completing an effective lesson plan.

Going into my classroom, I had teaching guides, but I will admit that my lesson plan was not what it should have been. However, that was no fault of my own. I had no idea

what to expect from the students; therefore, creating a plan
that would benefit each student was not possible prior to
knowing each and every child that walked into my classroom.
A good lesson plan includes all children, and creates ways to
teach each and every student. Getting to know the children
behind the desks in the classroom is one sure way to create a
lesson plan that not only benefits students inside of the
classroom, but it can benefit the students when they are
outside of the classroom as well. The lessons are there to
teach students, but there is a bigger purpose as well –
preparing students for life.

Having a lesson plan helped me "own" the subject that I
was teaching. Again, before I could create the lesson plan, I
had to realize the fundamental skills of each student in my
class; this is why a lesson plan will change year after year.
During my first year, I had to find a plan that would cater to
the students that I taught. In order to get my students to
engage in a classroom discussion, I used Martin Luther King,
Jr. speaking with a gang leader in the present day as a
stepping-stone, but this was not a method that I would use

every time. I would have to change up my teaching style,
which meant changing my lesson plan.

A good comparison for lesson planning is party planning.
The latter expands beyond a huge celebration; it includes
everything from a small family gathering, to a huge
retirement party for a co-worker or friend. The same skills
that planners use when planning a party can be used with
lesson planning. Teaching is truly fun, if the teacher allows it
to be. An educator's job should never be a chore; this will
have a negative impact on their lesson planning, teaching
methods, and the overall vibe of the classroom. I will explain
more about the benefits of having a positive classroom
environment in a future chapter.

Back to the party and lesson planning… Just like a party
requires planners to create activities that guests will enjoy,
and décor that coincides with a theme, a lesson plan requires
that same type of thought process. Teachers will need to
create lessons that engage their students, and plans that are

clear, and communicate exactly what it is that will help them reach a successful objective with their students.

When teachers begin creating an effective lesson plan, the biggest step within that process is to own it. This is true regardless if a teacher purchases a lesson plan online, or develops a plan from the beginning, all the way to the very end. Years ago, the question pertaining to whether or not a teacher should be allowed to post their lesson plan online was a big debate amongst administrators, parents, teachers, and other people around the world. Some teachers developed personal websites and posted their lesson plans online, free of charge. These free resources have become extremely popular.. This proves that a lesson plan is truly valuable when it pertains to teaching, as long as the plan outlines clear learning objectives and details to implement engaging learning activities.

Something that new teachers should never become accustomed to is purchasing a lesson plan and making no changes to that plan. I am positive that even though countless teachers obtain lesson plans online, a majority of them make changes to suit their teaching styles, and the learning styles of their students. Sure, teachers could use the lesson plans without making any changes, but how does that help their students? I already established what most teachers find out from the moment they step foot inside of their classroom – no one student is the same. However, teachers can find ways to help bridge the gaps between each student. Remember that a teacher is there to help their students learn, and that will require the educators to bring diversity into their classrooms, which includes their learning styles and techniques. When a teacher creates their own lesson plan, or makes changes to the lesson plan they have received via the internet, tailoring that lesson plan to meet the needs of each and every student is the first step in the right direction. Each teacher should own the content that they will teach students, and the teaching styles or methods that they plan to use.

Using another teacher's lesson plan is actually a good idea. It is important that teachers reach out to other teachers when working within an educational institution, and the prewritten lesson plan could be viewed as teacher collaboration. This book is meant to help teachers learn information that will help them out the moment they step foot inside of a classroom. The lesson plan obtained from another teacher could also prove to be an invaluable tool. A teacher should use a lesson plan, and this book, to improve their craft. The veteran teachers before me made mistakes, including their lesson plans, but after learning from those mistakes, they passed on knowledge to me as a new teacher. After learning techniques of my own, I passed that information on to other teachers. The lesson plans may need to be rewritten and planned in order to meet the needs of different students, but those lesson plans show teachers where to begin, instead of allowing a teacher to jump into the lesson planning stage without any assistance. However, a teacher must remember to make the lesson plan their "own," even if they are downloading a plan via the internet, or borrowing a lesson plan from another teacher.

Owning a lesson plan is a huge step in the right direction for many reasons. One of the reasons is because teachers are putting the thought and time into creating a lesson plan that will help their students – each and every one of them. Now this type of skill will not happen overnight; likewise, a teacher will not learn the students behind the desks in their classroom overnight. The lesson plans that teachers create will need to be altered each year; just like every event that a party planner plans will change. Themes change for parties, and the type of students that enter a classroom will change each year for a teacher. An example of this would be Candy Land… When I was a young student, this was a great approach. It really had me eager to learn more, and participate in the lesson. Do I believe this same idea would work today? Absolutely not! The style might, but the subject would not. With the creation of modern technologies, board games are almost a thing of the past, so teachers need to keep up with the times and create a lesson plan that reflects a more modern-day theme.

With the many issues that occur within urban communities, my MLK lesson was a great way to begin. The students in my classroom, and most classrooms within urban

communities, are affected by gang issues, regardless if that is
witnessing the gangs within their neighborhoods, being a part
of the gangs themselves, or having family members deeply
rooted within a gang. The bottom line was that everyone
could relate to that, and my classroom was the place where
my students could talk openly and freely about a matter that
impacted them on a daily basis. Allowing my students to
write about this gave them the extra privacy that they needed
to be one-hundred percent truthful about the matter, without
fearing any backlash. This method also allowed me to teach
the actual subject. This teaching method also allowed me to
get to know the students better, and that is what being a great
teacher is all about. A teacher cannot be the difference to a
student if they do not know the difference between their
students. Teachers need to know what makes each student
different, and how they can teach that individual student in a
clear, concise, and effective way.

A good lesson plan does not necessarily ensure that
students will learn what is intended, but the plan does make a
large contribution toward that goal. Lesson plans are without

a doubt an effective way to communicate with students. Every teacher should know that communication skills are fundamental, pertaining to teaching. In addition to communication, good lesson plans help each and every teacher organize materials, teaching methods, and content. The more teachers develop a lesson plan, the better at creating those plans they will be. Great lesson plans are necessary for all teachers, especially new and inexperienced educators. Remember how tightly I held on to my guide? What I truly needed was a great lesson plan that I myself had created.

There are unforeseen issues that come up all of the time, and this could cause teachers to be away from class for a day, week, month, or more. Disrupting students is never a good idea, which is why a great lesson plan is invaluable guidance for substitute teachers. This plan will help "save" students in case their teachers are unable to be in class to teach for whatever reasons. It also helps substitute teachers teach students according to how they learn, instead of following a guide that does not work well for each individual student.

As a new teacher, I learned that the lesson plan helped me just as much as it helped my students. It helped with my goal setting. If I needed to help my students learn subject matter, the plan would help me ensure that they were focused on the tasks that I had planned out each day, and it made sure that we had an effective plan in place to achieve those goals. Having the lesson plan helped me eliminate most of the procrastination that I, along with my students, had. Setting goals is how I stay organized year after year.

What a good lesson plan also helps me achieve is obtaining the necessary learning materials early on. What teachers in urban school systems learn quickly is that the resources and learning material available to students are not often up-to-par with what they should be. There are programs available that could potentially help teachers receive the educational resources that are necessary for their students to learn. Yes, this typically requires additional time, and it often requires a lot of hard work, but remember that teachers need to be the difference, and more often than not, that requires educators to go beyond normal classroom instruction. Reaching out to community leaders and program advisors in order to ensure students receive everything that they need to learn should not be a hindrance; it should be something that educators want to do.

I also learned that a good lesson plan helped me prevent indecisiveness. My lesson plan helped me prevent unnecessary problems from occurring as much as possible. Although an educator's teaching techniques should change as their students change, teachers do not want their routine to completely vanish into thin air. This often leads to procrastination and indecisiveness. Teachers need to change their routine in order to improve it; however, this should be done in an orderly manner. Most students in urban settings need a routine that they can follow; this routine will provide them with structure and balance.

I remember one of my students was a very good writer. Her name was Brandee. Remember her? She was the pregnant student who I had in my class for a short period of time. Brandee did not have all of the structural components

of an essay mastered, but she had great ideas, and she could
organize her thoughts beautifully. I believed that she was a
bright young lady, and with consistent support, she had a
bright future ahead of her. Had I stuck to my curriculum plan
without inviting my students to be a part of the planning
process, or changing the lesson plan to suit my students, I
may have never figured that out. I remember taking a risk
and abandoning my teacher's manual for my English
curriculum. We were supposed to cover the
comparison/contrast essay. My students were not interested
in answering the questions in the textbook, nor were they
interested in practicing similarities and differences. We
followed the same format every day: open your books, read
the passages, answer the questions, and write an essay with
your notes. This particular day, however, I brought in Black
Beat, Right On, and Word Up magazines. Teachers must
remember to relate to their students. After going to a local
Walgreens down the street from the school, in the inner city,
I was introduced to a whole section of magazines that I had
never even known existed. I had a feeling my students were

familiar with them. I used these pop culture magazines as a tool to cover my content. The students had to pick two pop idols and compare and contrast them. I was absolutely amazed by what the students wrote.

Brandee had great potential, and her essay stood out to me the most. Her essay was very good. She had compared Janet Jackson and Mary J. Blige. She talked about their beauty, style of music, popularity, and fame. Brandee concluded her essay by saying they both were her "she-roes" because they were living out their dreams. I was moved by her writing, and I learned a lot about her self-esteem and how she felt about being able to live out her dreams. Brandee's essay was a good way to speak with her about her writing skills and life. I let her know that things would be extremely hard for her with a baby, but that she had a lot of potential, and if she worked hard she could still try to go after her dreams. It was a very heartfelt conversation. Brandee cried like a baby, and I comforted her; in fact, I actually asked her if I could pray for her (taboo I know, but it was my real self). In that moment, I did what I felt led to do. I showed genuine

concern about a student. I made a strong connection with
Brandee, and that incident helped me develop my teaching
philosophy, which was to be a better teacher. I learned that I
had a better chance at meeting the curriculum goals by
getting to know my students, and tapping into their interests
and community resources. The more I did this, the easier it
became to teach.

Just like a well-planned party, a great lesson plan can
achieve success. An effective lesson plan helps teachers
communicate better, and an ineffective one does not. A great
lesson plan will incorporate the following things:

- Instructional procedures

- Student learning objectives

- Required educational materials

- A written description of how students will be
evaluated

Learning how to develop a good lesson plan will help contribute to the success of a teacher. New teachers will learn that lesson plans are indispensable. Educators will learn what it takes to "own" the subject matter and content that they are teaching. Teachers can analyze their lesson plan each year, and discover what worked well, what did not, and why. This allows teachers to go back and improve the lesson plan for future students. The most important benefits of a lesson plan are: helping each student learn effectively, as well as learning how to prepare for their future outside of the classroom.

Chapter 8:

Positive Classrooms Lead to Positive Outcomes

"Children learn and remember at least as much from the context of the classroom as from the content of the coursework." - Lawrence Kutner

Students learn more efficiently when they are in a positive classroom environment. It should be a teacher's priority to create a learning environment that leads to a successful and pleasurable learning atmosphere. I learned early on how impressionable children are. I also learned how sensitive students were to the other students around them, as well as the other teachers around them. Educators need to remember that students pick up very quickly on negativity, which could damage their self-esteem, and become a barrier to their emotional, intellectual, and social growth. This is one of the most important reasons why teachers need to create

and maintain a positive classroom environment for their
students.

I am glad that I look at each student as their own person.
So many teachers will alter their classrooms to suit a specific
type of student, and this should never be the case. Remember
the students I met on my first day; all of the children were
different, and unique. It was that uniqueness that made them
special, and their unique qualities are what would make them
stand out amongst other students as they continued on their
educational journey, and once they started their professional
careers. The first mistake a teacher can make is to lump
children into one category, and teach them according to what
others have said, or what other students before them have
done. That is a huge mistake, and it is not fair to any student.
This is also lazy, in terms of being a great teacher. As an
educator, getting to know the students behind the desk
should be a requirement, and teachers that fail to do so are
not only failing to be a difference in a student's life, but they
are failing to provide positive learning environments for the
children within their classrooms.

Keep in mind that students do not come to school each day hoping to disagree with teachers, or have an argument with their peers; instead, they want to come into a positive learning environment. The work in class should measure up with the students' capabilities, and the environment should be a positive one that the children will enjoy learning within. In today's society, a positive classroom is something that many students do not have the good fortune of experiencing – for different reasons.

Looking back at the Atlanta Public Schools (APS) cheating scandal; the children were the victims of practices and decisions made by adults. So many educators are more concerned with test scores and promotions that they do not put the needs of each child first, and ultimately, the children fail; therefore, the teacher fails. The social and emotional needs of each student should be addressed. These could be things that prevent the child from learning. In order for a student to receive a great education, all parties involved will need to do their part. This includes the students, parents,

teachers, school board, and other educational administrators
or staff members.

Although teachers cannot control what happens within
the homes of each student, or how the school board handles
curriculum, there are things that are within the control of
teachers, such as creating a positive learning environment for
their students. Educators have the ability to make the
classroom a place where students are eager to come into, and
a place that teaches students everything that they will need to
know about the current subject matter, as well as methods to
strive for greatness. This begins with providing support for
students, in addition to value, appreciation, and respect.
When teachers provide these things to their students, studies
have shown that learning comes more easily. Students who
have learning difficulties and personal challenges respond
better in a positive learning environment. When students are
inside of a positive classroom, they are not only physically
comfortable, but they have the emotional support that will
mentally motivate them to succeed.

Positive classrooms do more than help a student, these types of atmospheres help the teacher as well. As a new teacher, I had no idea where to begin, but I knew that I needed to be a positive force. I do not believe that all teachers set out to do negative things, but atmosphere could lead to those negative decisions and actions. The same is true with students in urban communities. Just because there are negative issues going on outside of the classroom, students are not waking up each day to add to them. Instead, they are searching for a way out; searching for a positive amongst all of the negatives. The classroom could be the positive that a student needs.

Do you believe the teachers involved in the APS scandal wanted to teach their students how to cheat? Do you believe they all had money on the brain? I honestly doubt that is the case. As I said previously, some teachers participated in the cheating scandal because they were afraid of losing their jobs, while other educators honestly felt they were helping the students succeed. In this case, there was not a positive

learning environment for the students, nor was there a
positive teaching environment for the teachers.

Part of creating a positive classroom is by shaping the
learning culture within the classroom. Teachers are
responsible for facilitating student learning, in addition to
making it possible for students to learn from each other.
Learning students will help teachers become more effective.
This also requires teachers to raise the expectations that they
have for their students. It is okay to push the students to do
more than is required of them. This is the type of motivation
that makes students want to do better. They know their
teachers have faith in them, and believe that they can achieve
greatness, which makes the students want to achieve that
greatness. This type of positivity is contagious, and it is
something that makes a great learning environment.

It is okay to develop rules for the classroom, but
remember that the rules should never be more important
than the students. There are ways to enforce rules without
lowering the level of respect students have for their teachers,

or their peers. When it is time to enforce discipline, teachers need to be positive at all times. A teacher can do so without compromising the level of respect or encouragement that they have for their students. Figure out what it is that makes the students act out. Perhaps the student does not feel a connection with their teacher, or with the class in general. A teacher should do what they can to fix that disconnect.

Educators want each child to feel significant, and they need to have a sense of belonging. Teachers should ask themselves if the type of discipline they have in place encourages good character. Teachers need to determine if their system teaches valuable social and life skills; if not, they need to reevaluate their disciplining techniques. Remember that teachers can discipline their students and maintain a positive classroom environment at the same time. The criteria that teachers use for discipline should encourage students to discover methods to use in order to develop their personal power and capabilities, in a constructive way. Discipline is not supposed to be negative; it was created to enforce positive values and lessons. It is also necessary to reinforce positive actions when they occur.

I often hear stories of children who "coin" another teacher as "strict." I myself have been referred to as strict. What I have learned is that teachers who are given the strict "title" also receive a stamp of approval. When the end of the year approaches, my students do not want to leave my class. Some are very emotional because they have grown to appreciate the "strict" teacher that I am. Often strict is viewed in a negative light, but that is something that a teacher has control of. Of course, there are strict teachers who do not care about their students, and they take the easy way out, instead of developing positive discipline methods. However, others find out why the student is being disruptive, and that teacher finds a way to handle the situation.

One issue that could disrupt a classroom is bad behavior. All students deserve to learn in a non-disruptive learning environment, and teachers are responsible for making sure that happens. When other students "act out," and disrupt the classroom, they will need to be disciplined, but in a positive way. Do not be under the misconception that a positive learning environment will automatically happen, because it will not. Teachers have to create that environment, and change the things that can be changed in order to achieve this.

When behavior problems occur, teachers try and diagnose the situation. This is never a good idea. Teachers look at their students and try to determine what is happening. Are students disruptive because they have poor attendance and they do not know what is going on in class when they attend? Do students from culturally diverse backgrounds lack the socially appropriate strategies for self-control and interpersonal interactions? Does the student who comes to school hungry disengage because his basic needs are not being met? Are some of the students just acting out in order to receive attention? Any attention is good in the eyes of a child that does not receive it outside of the classroom.

These are some of the questions that teachers ask; however, the important question is often overlooked. All of the questions mentioned in the previous paragraph somehow place the blame on the children for their behaviors. Do not misunderstand me, these may very well be important questions that need to be answered, but when diagnosing behavioral problems, a teacher must consider that he or she could be the problem. The teacher must look at what happens inside of their classroom and ask themselves, "Have I created a learning environment that engages all children in meaningful activities that support their learning?"

True, experienced teachers know that there might be at least one, two, or three students who chronically disrupt their classroom. Disruptive students come to class with challenging behavioral issues, and some students are difficult to deal with. A few students may even enjoy seeing their teachers get worked up. However, that does not mean that teachers should assume that they are not a part of the problem. Teachers will need to consider the deficiencies in the curriculum, instruction, and environment, instead of the deficiencies in the child. Educators must be willing to examine their own practices.

It is easy to recognize a positive learning environment by the classroom structure, relationships amongst students and teacher, and the climate for student success. Teachers can begin to establish a positive learning environment by following four steps: getting to know their students, establishing a positive culture, making learning relevant, and motivating students.

One teacher that I will never forget, Mr. Barker, disciplined his students in a positive way, but to a new teacher, it seemed as if it was negative discipline. I remember this instance as if it had occurred yesterday; it truly changed the way I viewed teaching. Being positive means helping students reach their true potential, instead of setting children up for failure. Teachers have a duty to motivate and teach students; teachers are not there to be best friends and timid.

The day that taught me a lot pertaining to disciplining students took place when I overheard the teacher, Mr.

Barker, speaking to his students. I was outside of his classroom, listening, as he was taking control of his class.

"I wouldn't take you around the corner with behavior like that," Mr. *Barker shouted as he slammed the door! "You kids think we are going on a field trip in three weeks and you can't even behave while we are in the building?" "Your behavior is absolutely unacceptable and you ought to be ashamed of yourselves."*

I listened to Mr. Barker go on and on for about three minutes. He was making point after point, and I thought this is insane. Should he be speaking to his students like this? Perhaps he should send them to the principal's office. While I was thinking of ways that Mr. Barker could solve the behavioral issues in his class, I heard him begin to speak up again. This time, he told the students to take out their math books and put them on their desks. I peeked into the classroom and noticed that he was looking around the room. I, like Mr. Barker, noticed that only twelve out of the 25 students had their books. Mr. Barker told the twelve students who had their books to stand up.

"Thank you all for coming to class prepared. You all are on the right track. You came to school and you came prepared to learn. I am so proud of you."

One of his students, Tracey, interrupted, "See Mr. B, what had happened was I was finna get my book and bring it, den my phone started rangin' and it was my puppy and I was like OMG my puppy can talk!"

Mr. Barker had a stern look on his face and said, "Tracey, stop acting so silly all of the time. You are not funny. You have an excuse every other day. You are never going to get anywhere in life like this. Sit down, close your mouth, take out some paper, and focus on what we are doing in here. You have to want to make it girl; I can't do that part for you."

You could hear a pin drop on the floor, and just like that, class officially started. In particular, the scene in Mr. Barker's classroom might not appear to be caring to an outside observer; however, his classroom represented the dynamics that many African American teachers are known to have with their African American students. Many are very vocal about their expectations and helping students see that they have no time to waste in school. They take charge in their classrooms, as each teacher should, as long as it is beneficial to the students, and the classroom environment.

I had students who wanted to go to the principal's office, instead of staying in class and actually doing real work. In these instances, I was not disciplining my students; I was doing exactly what they wanted. This is why it is important for teachers to handle their own discipline issues, unless there is something that is beyond their control, such as fighting. Students learned to respect me more when I disciplined them on my own; they knew that while I would be a positive figure in their lives, I would not tolerate nonsense within my classroom. Some of the methods I used to discipline my students included "detention centers" in class. Once students were ready to get back on track and become successful inside of the classroom, I would allow them to leave the detention center program I had created.

When promoting positive discipline, a teacher must be clear about their expectations for the class, and make sure that those expectations are in a place that is visible for students to see – state those expectations in a positive manner to students as well. When students follow the guidelines of the classroom, teachers should recognize the students, especially when a student that was once disruptive stops those disruptive patterns in class.

It is crucial that teachers work together in order to provide their students with a positive classroom. Some of the students that teachers will come into contact with have been neglected, abused, or suffer from extreme academic, emotional, and social issues. Some of the students that I have taught over the years had transferred from one school to another, countless times. Living in a low-income community means that the students in urban schools often come from disadvantaged backgrounds. This is why it is critical that all teachers work together to help ensure that students walk into a positive learning environment each day. If teachers support one another, their students will see this positive behavior, and it will encourage them to work with their peers.

Teachers who take the time to get to know the students behind the desks, and work with other teachers, have the ability to provide students with a positive classroom environment. My students would often ask me why I taught at my school. My main reason was because it was where I was needed and could make a difference. Many of my students did not have the same advantages that students from middle-class and upper-class families had, and I felt obligated to give my students the best education possible so that they could make opportunities for themselves as they got older. Teaching in an urban school is very rewarding, and even on the most stressful days, I go home knowing that I am making a difference in the lives of my students.

Chapter 9:

Supportive Teachers Provide Supportive Learning Environments

"You need an attitude of service. You're not just serving yourself. You help others to grow up and you grow with them." — David Green

Teachers need to be supportive of their students, but teachers deserve some support in return, and it is there. Support not only comes from the parents within the community, the students in a classroom, or the friends and family in a teacher's personal life; that support also comes from colleagues. Teachers are there to uplift students, as well as each other. However, it is up to the teacher to utilize the help that is available in order to do their job more effectively, and more efficiently.

On my first day as a new teacher, I remember feeling as if I was left alone to do my job, without help from anyone.

The truth was, while some of the administrators and staff members were too busy to help me out, there were other teachers who would have allowed me to lean on them throughout my first year, and the many years that followed. Teachers cannot transform the classrooms within the urban school systems if they do not work with each other. Working against one another does not provide a positive learning environment for students, nor does it provide teachers with a positive working environment.

Sometimes the day would take its toll on me; I would need courage to make it through that day, and the strength to come into school the next day. Teachers are constantly in the public eye, and they have a difficult job that has the ability to affect the course of a child's life. Just like their students, teachers experience many challenges. Teaching is often a stressful job, which is why teacher collaboration and support is necessary in every learning environment. Studies show that the turnover rate for schools where teachers have a great support system is low, in comparison to educational institutions where teacher support or mentoring programs are not offered.

I wish I could take this time to apologize to my former students, especially on those days when I may not have had the courage that I longed for, as well as those times when I made mistakes. Teachers do not want to let their students down; this is never a teacher's objective. When individuals become teachers, a majority do so because they want to help others become great. Teaching is a job where someone has the ability to be a deciding factor in how much a student learns, and how well that student uses what he has learned to become a positive part of the world that he lives in.

The fact remains that teachers are going to make mistakes; it is inevitable. Regardless of how well someone studies in college, or how many "How to Guides" they read, mistakes are still going to happen. The good thing about mistakes is that people can learn from them. There were so many errors that I made during my first few years as a teacher, but I took those mistakes as lessons, and vowed to do better so that I could be the difference for my future students. I increased the amount of time I spent on creating classroom lessons, and I learned to develop classroom expectations, as well as methods to continue on when I did not meet those expectations. Teachers need to learn how to broach their expectations of students in order to prevent things from spiraling during the school year.

From the moment I stepped into the classroom, I was making a lifelong commitment to the students who would walk through my doors. I had to commit to learning, which meant learning my students, learning how to become a successful teacher, and learning how to use the support systems that were around me. I learned year after year how to be a better teacher, and in the process, my students had a teacher that was not only working hard to teach them what they needed to learn, but a teacher who would do whatever she had to do in order to be a difference in their lives. I now see those mistakes as an opportunity to learn; all teachers should do this, while remaining committed to their students.

I remember when I was teaching the students in my backyard. I did not do this because I had to; I did it because I wanted to. I felt the need and desire to help others feel great about learning, just as I had felt. I was not vulnerable; I was eager to teach. This is the same attitude I should have had in the classroom as a new teacher, but that was not always possible. Becoming a great teacher is a learning process, and teachers have to learn just as much as students. A teacher must also be prepared to lean on other people. After all, when someone learns from their mistakes, this will require involvement from other people.

When I decided that teaching was the only job for me, I was only concerned with helping others be great. I never became a teacher because I wanted to earn a paycheck, or because I wanted to teach students in the wealthiest school districts. I wanted to help change the lives of my students, and motivate them to be the best that they could be. I quickly learned that this was easier said than done, but with commitment, and the ability to reach out to parents and other teachers, I could do this. Regardless of how bad things may seem, teachers need to remain positive and focused.

As I said, I made a lot of mistakes, but each year, I tried to correct those mistakes and become a better teacher. Teachers do the very best that they can, and sometimes teachers try to do too much without relying on others for assistance. There were some teachers that did not have great reputations within the schools where I was teaching, so I never thought to go to them for help. I decided to learn as much as I could on my own, instead of reaching out. Being the "new kid on the block" is something that many teachers experience, and they avoid seeking help for many reasons, such as fear of losing their jobs, or fear of losing the respect of other teachers. These are not thoughts that an educator should have, but unfortunately, many do.

When colleagues do not welcome others, it is hard to rely on that person for support going forward. However, teachers must be the support group that students need. This type of support is not only great for the students, but it is detrimental to new and inexperienced teachers. One cannot get better without support and hard work. Teachers who isolate themselves from other teachers are not helping anyone involved, especially their students. Teachers should always open their door to receive help, and make sure that their door is open to help other teachers. Educators need to remember that teaching students is not one person's job; it requires teamwork. The phrase "team work makes the dream work" is accurate on many levels, and teaching is one of them.

I had a great "teacher-partner" that was so helpful to me. Her name was Mrs. Richie, and she came into my classroom without being invited. She introduced herself, and offered to help me transition into my job. I remember looking up at her, dazed and confused. I had never had this happen before, so I did not know how to respond. I remember coming to, and being so happy that she had walked into my classroom. She had been teaching at our school for eight years, and she offered her wisdom and experience to me. She gave me suggestions and teaching methods to use in order to straighten up my class, and encourage them to succeed. I knew from the moment that I met Mrs. Richie she would be a great teacher-partner, and she was. From that day forth, she gave me the support that I needed, and I gave her support in return. I find myself being "Mrs. Richie" for other teachers; helping them out just like my first teacher-partner had done for me.

Support also extends beyond the school building; there are community leaders who support teachers, as well as the parents of students. I have met so many great parents over the years, and this led me to use what is known as a "parent-partner." We work together to make sure their child is receiving the best education, and we develop ways to make the student's learning experience as effective and positive as possible. If I have an issue where the student does not want to learn – believe me, there are many of those instances – my parent-partner will assist me to help the student do better inside of the classroom.

In one specific instance, a student, Shanta, kept giving me a hard time. Finally, I realized I would need assistance, so I reached out to her mother. My colleagues said that it would be a complete waste of time, but I did it anyway. I thought back to how I was somewhat of a "class clown," but the thought of my teachers calling my parents would straighten me up. When I reached out to Shanta's mother, I did not receive a call back from her immediately. After a while, I thought that the other teachers were right, and it was a complete waste of time. It turns out that Shanta's mother did not receive my message, because her job did not allow personal phone calls. If I had not taken another course of action to contact her, I would have never known that Shanta's mother was just like my mom had been when I was a child; willing to do whatever to help my teachers by being their biggest supporter. Shanta's mother cared a great deal – as most of the parents do – and she was willing to help me keep her daughter in line while she was in class, and help Shanta remain focused outside of the classroom as well.

This instance taught me a great deal pertaining to parent involvement. Shanta's home phone was disconnected, which is why I had to use another method to contact her mother. I had reached out via postal mail when the message left at her workplace was not passed along. Teachers need to be aware that contacting a parent is not always the easiest thing to do, but parent involvement is extremely important. For this reason, teachers must be cultured, and willing to work hard so that they can form closer ties with the parents of their students. Parent involvement could help a student work more diligently in class, and it could cause a student's academic performance to improve.

To be an effective teacher, teaming up with other teachers, parents, and community leaders is necessary. All teachers must take the time to commit to students in order to help them succeed. It was my job as a teacher to find the support that I needed, but as a new teacher, I failed to do this. Looking back, I wish that I had made that commitment. It would have benefited me, and it would have also had a great impact on my students. I want all teachers to know that even though they teach, they will learn a lot on their journey as an educator. All teachers can do is their best, and remain focused and supportive of their students, other teachers, and those working to help transform the classrooms.

CHAPTER 10:

COMMITMENT, INSPIRATION, AND DEDICATION

"By learning you will teach; by teaching you will understand." - Latin Proverb

There are many challenges associated with teaching in an urban school, but there are just as many benefits teaching in an urban school system. Many students living in low-income communities need a teacher who is willing to go that extra mile and truly be a difference in their lives. When we sign up to be teachers, we are signing up to be that person that students can count on, regardless of colors and characteristics. Each child comes to school to learn, and to be given the same opportunity as all students. The American values that make this world so great are the same American values that we should teach to our students.

All teachers need to be committed to the success of their students, regardless if they are a veteran educator, or a new teacher. From the moment I stepped foot into my classroom, I knew that I wanted to be a difference in the life of each student who walked through my door. There were times when I believed I would not make it, and I thought about relocating to another school system – one that was within a more privileged community. However, those thoughts left my mind when I realized that I could not walk out on the children in my classroom. I owed them the right to receive the motivation necessary to have a bright future. I owed it to my students to remain committed; suddenly, the challenges associated with being a teacher seemed small in comparison.

Motivating a student on his or her success is not the only thing that I had to do. I had to believe what I was doing. Many people doubt the level of knowledge that students have, but it is true that they know more than we give them credit for. My students were extremely smart, and they knew the difference between motivation and spoken words. The latter is saying something over and over; this does not mean those words are something that the speaker believes; they are purely spoken words. However, motivation is only given when a person feels that something is attainable. If I did not believe in my students, they would have known. The truth is, I believed in each and every student that walked through my door on the first day of class, and I still have that same belief in all of the students that I have had the honor of teaching throughout my career. My students all work hard to keep up with the lessons that I teach, and they work hard to learn more for themselves. Sure, there are some students that need a little more motivating than others, but they all want to learn – some just need more of a push.

Being dedicated to the success of my students was something that I had to become immediately. I knew that my students would feed off of my lead. If I was dedicated to them, they would also be dedicated to themselves. Hard work and dedication go hand-in-hand, regardless if those actions are associated with school, a career, or life in general. All of the great things that people achieve in life cannot be obtained without hard work and dedication. This is something that I drilled into the brains of my students on a regular basis. However, it did not matter how much I said it, unless the students could see me living it. If I came to school and taught a lesson one day, and then allowed my students to go an entire day without learning the next, was I really dedicated? Did I truly value the future of my students? The answer is no. While I am a teacher, and as a teacher, I should make learning fun, the point is that the students need to learn. A teacher should never become complacent in regards to a student's education.

Inspiring students to learn is a challenge that I meet year after year. My students are not motivated to learn because they have to, they are motivated to learn because they want to. This is the difference between teachers who inspire, and educators who simply want to collect a paycheck. When a person wakes up and goes to work, they do so because they have to earn a living in order to survive. The person does not necessarily go to work because they want to. When students complete their work in unpleasant circumstances, under the tutelage of uninspiring teachers, they are not motivated.